ISBN 978-0-243-95303-5
PIBN 10139366

1 MONTH OF
FREE
READING

at

www.ForgottenBooks.com

By purchasing this book you are eligible for one month membership to ForgottenBooks.com, giving you unlimited access to our entire collection of over 1,000,000 titles via our web site and mobile apps.

To claim your free month visit:

www.forgottenbooks.com/free139366

English
Français
Deutsche
Italiano
Español
Português

www.forgottenbooks.com

Mythology Photography **Fiction**
Fishing Christianity **Art** Cooking
Essays Buddhism Freemasonry
Medicine **Biology** Music **Ancient
Egypt** Evolution Carpentry Physics
Dance Geology **Mathematics** Fitness
Shakespeare **Folklore** Yoga Marketing
Confidence Immortality Biographies
Poetry **Psychology** Witchcraft
Electronics Chemistry History **Law**
Accounting **Philosophy** Anthropology
Alchemy Drama Quantum Mechanics
Atheism Sexual Health **Ancient History**
Entrepreneurship Languages Sport
Paleontology Needlework Islam
Metaphysics Investment Archaeology
Parenting Statistics Criminology
Motivational

MANLINESS.

FOR YOUNG MEN

AND THEIR WELL-WISHERS.

BY

REV. B. B. HOTCHKIN.

———•••———

PHILADELPHIA:

PRESBYTERIAN BOARD OF PUBLICATION

1334 CHESTNUT STREET.

STEREOTYPED BY WESTCOTT & THOMSON.

MANLINESS.

PART I.

AWAY FROM HOME.

Two lads met on the public grounds, in the rear of the City Hall in New York. One of them was employed in a shipping house on the East River; the other was a clerk in Pearl street. Both were from the country. They had been neighbours there, and they were fellow boarders now. In age, one was a few days past eighteen: the other, a few weeks short of that mark.

In New York there was for them nothing which met their need of home. They had been allowed thus early to pass out from those influences with which the presence of good parents, brothers and sisters, always surrounds the youth whom God favors with pleasant kindred and a happy home. God, who arranges all the natural changes in our lives, has fixed the period when it is safe for us to assume the whole care of ourselves.

Perhaps these lads had become impatient of this arrangement, and had left home because they were tired of being children, and wished to become men before God's appointed time.

I have known many lads who, for just this reason, have sought employment far out of sight of their nearest kindred—far out of reach of the gentle, restraining influence of home. In after life, they have reviewed this perilous choice with very different feelings.

God made us all to be happy, only as we fall in with his own good arrangements for our comfort. He has fitted each period in our lives to afford some peculiar joy which belongs to that period, but which, if then lost, can never afterward be secured. Of all the pleasures born of earth, none is more pure and satisfying than that of a child during the years while he is a child. So also there are peculiar susceptibilities of joy for the transition age where the borders of childhood and youth meet. There is a sweet beauty in the blithesomeness of either boy or girl, growing up happy, good and pure.

The goodness of this arrangement is not apt to be estimated until long after years. The time, however, comes when those who have lost their childhood, reflect upon their loss. The time comes when they would give every later joy of life for the recovery of what was then lost.

Sometimes the loss is altogether a misfortune, a dark and distressing dispensation from the hand of God. The boy had no home to dwell in, and no friends to love. On earth there were no hearts to receive his young affections. A mournful lot—what pity the mention of it should awaken in all our breasts!

I saw one such die in the hospital in Hagerstown, where I was spending a few weeks in the service of the United States' Christian Commission. He was a boy soldier, scarcely eighteen years old, delicate in frame, and with a countenance which I thought must have been habitually sad. I did not see it until the hand of death was upon it. Sense, voice, and breath were almost gone. "My poor boy! where is your home?" I asked him. His articulation was thick, low and broken. With my ear close by his lips, I made out the

1 *

reply—"*Wherever night overtakes me.*" I afterward learned more of him from a fellow soldier who knew his past life. *What he had told me was literally true.* His whole childhood had been a homeless, and hence a joyless one. No mother had taught him how to live, or how to die.

Others have made the voluntary sacrifice of their boyhood. They surrendered the delights and safeguards which God spreads only before ripening, but not ripe youthfulness be cause they were in haste for the dignities and wearing cares of manhood. The time comes for them to know what they have lost. Strong and stern men, upon whose heads the storms of life have beat until they were bowed under sorrows and years, while reviewing this costly sacrifice of their early days, have thought with unavailing tears—"Oh that 1 were once more a little child! Then I would again lay my troubles on my mother's heart, and while I sobbed upon her breast, she would sing me to sleep, and I should awake *so* happy!"

Perhaps the young men of whom I now write, had been led by weariness of boyhood and its proper restraints, to abandon their country homes. Perhaps, on the other hand, there was better cause for their coming to the city. Be this as it may, they had left all the friends and associations of their childhood, and had assumed alone the solemn charge of taking care of themselves in this perilous world. Well, they are candidates for manhood now. All who love the young because Christ loved them, will inquire with earnest interest how they progress.

It was evening twilight, after a pleasant day in early autumn, when they met as already stated, in the rear of the City Hall. HARFRANT, who had been longest in the city, accosted his fellow boarder :—

"Where away now, WILL?"

"Nowhere in particular," was the response.

" Out for a walk, eh? What are you going to do with yourself all the evening ?"

" Oh I shall go to Mrs. Kramer's* after a little turn. They make a pleasant family sit-down there, and I often spend my evenings with them. It is more like home than anything else which I find in this New York wilderness."

" Come with me to-night, Will : I will show

* Their boarding-place.

you something better than a family sit-
down."

"Where?"

"At the National. Burton performs in
'The Serious Family.'* If you want to see
our old psalm-singing neighbors riddled, there
is the place. Your Deacon Goodwalk could
not whine it off more to the life. Say, will
you go?"

"I think not."

"Yes you will. Come along!"

"I believe I will not go to-night."

"Why not to-night? You have not been
to the theatre for an age : at least I have not
known of your going. In fact I do not know
that I ever saw you there. I tell you what,
Will, I begin to suspect—but tell me now—
honor bright!—were you *ever* at the theatre?"

"Supposing I have not been"—

"Supposing you have not been!† Why,

---

* "The National" was a theatre. The play of "The Serious Family" was a burlesque of household religion. With
Burton for buffoon, it had, a number of years ago, what is
called " a run."

† In giving this conversation I choose to omit the fearful
profanity which the speaker now began to use. If the
reader ever felt the chill which I always experience on hear-

what is the use of coming to New York to live? '*Supposing you have not been!*' Supposing you have been humdrumming between your store and Mrs. Kramer's, with an extra turn to church on Sundays, these six months, and your eye teeth not yet cut! Supposing you daren't go because you haven't asked pa and ma, and they wouldn't let you if you should, for Deacon Goodwalk would be over the next day to church them! *Supposing you are too chicken-hearted to be a man!*"

Will was beginning to exhibit embarrassment. He was perfectly aware that the manner in which his companion assailed his reluctance from the theatre, was beneath contempt. But who can measure the power of false shame?

The quick discernment of Harfrant had caught his want of manly courage to return a blunt "No!" to the question whether he had ever been at the theatre. He observed in the irresolute workings of his mind the symptom that he had neither the wisdom to fly from temptation, nor the strength to face it. Seeing this, he did what any dextrous

ing the language in which profane sinners speak of sacred names and things, he will be grateful for this omission.

agent of Satan would have done under the same circumstances—he crowded him harder.

"Will," said he, "you are a fine fellow: we all know that. But you are a *little* verdant yet. You must learn some things, or you will not do to live in New York. It takes a *man* to get along here. I will not ask you again whether you have attended the theatre, for I see you have not, and you do not quite like to own it. And you have never made the acquaintance of the fellows at Wilson's, eh?"

Wilson's was a house where a club made up chiefly from young clerks, resorted for carousal and gambling. Will did not immediately reply to the last question, and his companion resumed:—

"I see how it is. But never mind! you have the right stuff in you when you are once started, and you shall be a man yet. I suppose too you have never been down —— street, eh?"*

The color mounted to Will's face. It was a flush of honest indignation. He felt an insult in the bare question, and the first im-

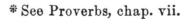

* See Proverbs, chap. vii.

pulse of his heart was to resent it as it deserved. But the cool hardened eye of Harfrant was more than a match for this virtuous prompting. Again he quailed before the tempter. True he did reply, "No;" but *so* timidly! Neither voice nor look met the occasion.

"Then, Will," said Harfrant, this time throwing something of scorn into his tone, "in the name of all that is wide awake, *where have you been?* O I forget: at Mrs. Kramer's family sit-down. All very well for a boy! but when are you going to be a man? By-the-bye you *have* been at Barker's, for I saw you coming out. Well, that is something."

Barker's was a saloon for drinking, smoking, and playing billiards. It was called a genteel establishment; but few ever became familiar guests there, without passing on to those more loathsome dens of vice from which Will had thus far been preserved. To the intimation that he had visited Barker's he briskly replied,

"Yes, several times."

Here one secret of his moral weakness was out. *He had begun to go wrong.* This largely accounts for the failure of virtuous courage to come to the rescue, throughout this whole conflict with temptation. He had passed over to the enemy's ground, and under those disadvantages of position the battle was being fought.

Now the truth was, Will had been at Barker's only twice. A fellow clerk, representing it as a genteel place where all the *young gentlemen* go, had prevailed on him to go in. It was less than a week since his first visit there, but he had already brought away the mark. That mark was on his soul. He was not like an old drinker whose bodily strength is broken, and whose limbs shake when he attempts to move. But the strength of his soul was impaired, and his moral courage shook before the tempter.

The most fearful moral symptom disclosed in this whole interview, was that while he acknowledged, with evident hesitation, that he had *not* been at the theatre and certain other gateways of perdition, he was anxious to make the most of his two calls at Barker's. As before stated, they were only two, yet there seemed to be a relief from embarrassment in the answer, " Yes, several times." He seemed to expect that this would somewhat redeem his character in the eyes of his companion, who had begun to make him feel that it was *rather* boyish to consume his evenings at Mrs. Kramer's, when all New York was before him.

" Come then !" said Harfrant, " we will go to the performance at the National to-night," laying his hand as he spoke, within the other's elbow.

But the conquest of Will was not complete. He stood thoughtfully a few moments, slowly withdrew his arm from Harfrant, and *began* to turn away.

Was he saved ?

I have sometimes thought that when parents forsake the control of their children before it is proper to commit them to the perils of self-government, God looks upon those forsaken ones with peculiar sympathy and care. I have inquired wondering, Does he not then send one of the most gentle and loving of his angels, to become the guardian of the early wanderer in this world of peril; to be his silent and unseen protector by day; to hover about his pillow by night; and to breathe into his soul lovely thoughts of his childhood's

2

home, and still lovelier thoughts of his Father in heaven?

Not long since, from my window, I saw a prowling cat creeping through the grass of a summer lawn, toward a young robin that was too soon out of its nest. The parent bird saw the peril of her birdling, but she was powerless for rescue. She did all that she could: she flew wildly about, sending out in swift sharp chirps her shrill note of alarm. But the tigress, heedless of her agony, and intent only on the marked victim, crawled up furtive and slow, until her range was reached: then came one fatal spring, and her fangs were fastened in her prey. Then a wilder shriek of distress came from the mother, and on the wing she mounted away from the scene where the call for her care was past.

So my fancy has pictured the unprotected youth, when the glaring eyes of the tiger, temptation, who is creeping stealthily toward him, have marked him for ruin. I have thought that the unseen guardian from heaven was then flying around him in compassionate alarm, warning him of the murderous peril at hand, and calling him to escape as a bird from the fowler's snare. But if the prey has at last been struck, I have thought of that faithful watcher as turning away with a cry of anguish, on finding that her anxious care has been vain, and ascending with the report, "He is gone!"

Will was now so far cowered under the taunts of Harfrant, that he was ashamed to acknowledge the reluctance which he really felt toward vice. Still he withheld his consent from accompanying him to the theatre.

Was there not a celestial spirit near him then, calling to his memory the old songs of home—that home where parents, brothers, and sisters, would turn pale on hearing that he had hearkened to scorners, and sold himself to perdition? Did she not speak to him of the happiness of those pleasures of early years, which brought no remorse? And did she not also tell him that this was a happiness to which he could never return, and feel in it what he once felt, after breathing the air of such abodes of corruption as he was now urged to enter? Did she not farther speak to him of the great and good Father in heaven, who loves those that love him, and whose smile is worth more than the approval of millions of creatures like Harfrant? And did she not tell him that this holy Father on high could never behold him in smiling love, while he plainly showed that he cared more for the scorn of one scoffing sinner, than for the approval of Heaven?

We should expect in Will the best effect from these tender suggestions, if we could discover, through his conduct, more exhibition of moral strength. More certainly we should expect it, if we could know that he was supplicating God for such strength. For apart from this Divine aid, no one has power in this soul's life-and-death conflict.

But there is poor relief for our apprehensions, in this movement of slowly beginning to turn from the tempter. True it was a turning-away movement, and so far it was good and hopeful. But it lacked promptness; it was irresolute, and so far it was bad. It was just the emergency in which those who hesitate are oftener lost than saved. He should not have stood a moment. It required but an instant to know what was right. He should have hastened away. It was in such a moment of peril that Bunyan's pilgrim, stopping both ears with his hands, ran from the tempter crying, "*Life! Life! Eternal Life!*"

Harfrant saw, in the tardiness of Will's movement, the absence of any well-resolved purpose, and this prompted another effort to secure him. Stepping after him, and laying his hand on his shoulder, he said :—

"Oh pshaw, Will! this is childish. One would think that your mother's apron strings reach all the way from Fairstream to New York. Come now! when do you expect to be anybody at this rate? Be a man, Will! *Be a man!*"

"Be a man!" A sublime call worthy of heaven, here sent up from hell! Did it accomplish the purpose of hell?

Patience, reader! The end of this conflict for a soul has not yet come.

Oh, it was a fearful hour for the lone youthful wrestler against the adversary! Our interest in the conflict deepens, when we behold the ground over which it is fought as reduced simply to this—his fear that he might become unmanly, or rather that his associates might treat him as cowardly, and fit only for the leading strings of a child. It does not appear that he had any taste for the theatre, or

2*

any desire to hear his father's psalm-singing neighbors burlesqued in the play of "The Serious Family." Left to himself, he would probably have preferred the family circle at Mrs. Kramer's. But how was he to stand before the taunt of cowardice? How resist, when, among associates whose scorn would become intensely annoying, his manliness was at stake?

It is easy for us, who are coolly reading the account of his peril, to see the points in which he failed. But the attack was pressed upon him rapidly: no time was allowed him for reflection. He should have refused to be pushed headlong by a motive, until he had thought for himself whether the inducement was lawful and good, and especially whether it was applied fairly to the present case. He should have considered what true manliness is, and whether that which Harfrant so urgently proposed, was a real or false manhood. He should have reflected whether it was probable that the theatre and other throne-chambers of vice, would make a man of him. He should have looked upon his companion, so early hardened, and pluming himself upon his premature initiation into vice, and he should then have judged for himself whether, by following such an example, he was likely to become worthier of the noble title of MAN.

Above all he should have remembered that God can instantly hear the praying desire, sent up in the moment of need; and he should have lifted his heart to him in earnest prayer that he might be saved in the dark hour of temptation. For thus our Saviour has himself taught us to pray—"Lead us not into temptation, but deliver us from evil."

This last he certainly did not do. Was he lost?

*　　*　　*　　*　　*　　*

Suddenly, and as if from the clouds, a third person appeared at their side.

He was not however a celestial visitant, but a plain and good man of earth, coming in with heavenly intent—one who, in good time, will become a real angel. As a gentleman and man of business, he enjoyed what he deserved—a good amount of public esteem. But better than this, he was one of the working Christians of New York, who are in earnest strife with the powers of evil to seek and save the lost. In the Sabbath School, and in an Association for the benefit of inexperienced young men from abroad, he had often encountered cases which illustrate the perils of city life to youth from the country; and he had learned to feel a peculiar anxiety for such cases of exposure. He was a worshipper in the church which Will attended, in company with the family of Mrs. Kramer. Thus the lad was already known to him by sight; but he was not acquainted with his position in the city, or his need of some sympathizing Christian counsellor, until he had heard what had just passed.

He was sitting on the steps of the old building in the rear of the City Hall, enjoying the evening breeze, when, as already told, the fellow boarders met. He was near enough to hear their conversation, and to observe that one of the speakers was the youth whose fine honest countenance had engaged his attention in church, and in whose behalf a silent interest had already grown up in his heart. He listened with loathing to the coarse and profane scoffs of Harfrant; but when he saw that the net of false shame was gathering closer and closer around the perplexed boy, he felt his heart almost bursting its walls, so strong were the throbbings of anxiety there. " I can never forgive myself," he said to himself, " if I see that poor lad led as an ox to the slaughter, without one resolute effort to save him." He stepped out before the youngsters, and in a tone of affectionate earnestness, said to Will :

" My young friend, you are now deciding a very solemn question. It may be the turning point for your life and your eternity. Will you hear me a moment ?"

" Who are *you?* and what business have you to interfere ?" growled Harfrant.

" Who I am, is nothing to *you* at present," replied the gentleman, and then added : " But I shall take the liberty to interfere in behalf of that manhood, in the name of which you would rob a fellow youth of the last shred of manliness."

" What is he to you ?"

The question was accompanied by a volley of coarse and profane epithets : God forbid that I should write them ! The gentleman answered :

" He is to me one whom I have seen in the house of God ; and he is one for whom, though unknown by name, I have offered the prayer that I may hereafter see him in the sanctuary on high."

"Who asked for a preachment?"

"You asked a question, and you shall have an answer, call it preachment, or whatever you will. He is to me one for whom I feel a newly awakened anxiety, because of what I have just heard. For I learn from your conversation, that he is alone amid the dangers of unguarded and inexperienced youth. I now see him, like Daniel, in the den of lions. But I have no assurance that he is, as Daniel was, safe from the teeth of the monsters; for I do not know whether he loves the God whom Daniel loved, or whether he prays to him who heard Daniel's prayer."

Another interruption, accompanied with profane scoffs, was attempted. The gentleman gave it no attention, but went on:

"Your brutal sneers about his mother's apron strings, his psalm-singing neighbours, and Deacon Goodwalk, inform me that he has a far-off home, and that holy influences surround that home. There, from beside the cradle of his infancy, prayer probably ascended. There loving hearts still dwell— hearts in which his own earliest love was treasured, and which are now watching, with intense affection, for his well-doing. There gray hairs will be brought down in sorrow to the grave, if you should succeed in persuading him to enter the gates of ruin. There are clustered a world of gentle affections which he may bless, if he becomes a true man, or which he will crush, if he destroys himself."

The running fire of profanity and scurrility which Harfrant had kept up, from the first moment of this gentleman's appearance, gradually fell off into a low murmur, addressed to Will, "Come, let's go! Come on! Come!"

But Will felt himself held by the earnest sympathy of his new and strangely found friend. In the voice of the latter there was a tone which fastened him. He could not flee.

What had just been said to Harfrant, was not for the thankless sake of replying to him. The speaker meant to touch a chord in the heart of the tempted lad, to which the feelings of man will respond as long as the soul is alive to any human affection.

O the talismanic power of that one word, Home!

The late Dr. Bethune, in relating some
incidents of his early experience as a preacher
to seamen, told of an old Scotch sailor who
lay in Charleston, sick unto death. He had
lived a long life of sin, and now, face to face
with death, he was still careless respecting
the fate of his soul. Conversation after conversation passed; but he heard, with stolid
indifference, respecting the love of Christ, the
eternal heaven, and the dark realm of the
lost.

One day the minister, a part of whose own
early years had been spent in Scotland, sang
in his hearing a verse of one of the cradle
songs which he knew were frequently used
by Scotch mothers, in the common rank of
life.

In an instant, the dying man's attention
was excited. He listened: the tide of feeling
in his bosom welled up and overflowed. The
days, the parents, the friends, the prayers,
and all the sacred things of childhood, passed
in review. The memories thus awakened by
one stanza from a Scottish mother's lullaby,
stirred the sensibilities which had slept under
all the artillery of eternal truth.

Cowper, the many mournful passages of

whose future life were traceable to the early loss of both mother and home, long years afterward thus wrote of that home then broken up, and that mother gone :—

" Where once we dwelt, our name is heard no more.
Children, not thine, have trod my nursery floor.
And where the gardener, Robin, day by day,
Drew me to school along the public way,
Delighted with my bauble coach, and wrapped
In scarlet mantle warm, and velvet capped,
'Tis now become a history little known,
That once we called the pastoral house our own.

" Short lived possession ! but the record fair,
That memory keeps of all thy kindness there,
Still outlives many a storm, that has effaced
A thousand other themes less deeply traced.
Thy nightly visits to my chamber made,
That thou mightst know me warm and safely laid;
Thy morning bounties ere I left my home—
The biscuit, or confectionary plum;
The splurging waters on my cheeks, bestowed
By thy own hand, till fresh they shone and glowed:
All this, and more endearing still than all,
Thy constant flow of love, that knew no fall;
All this, still legible on memory's page,
And still to be so to my latest age,
Adds joy to duty, makes me glad to pay
Such honors to thee as my numbers may."

In the case of Will, there were symptoms that the appeal to home memories was not all lost. His attention was secured, and this

3

was something gained. But whether he could be persuaded to break from the snare closing around him, was yet to be seen. The gentleman who had stepped into the arena, intent on his rescue, now laying his hand kindly on the lad's shoulder, and addressing himself directly to him, inquired :—

"What would your companion have? He asks you to become a man, and that is what you wish, is it not?"

Will nodded assent.

"I suppose his present persuasions would have no influence with you, but for his promise that if you will follow his lead, he will make a man of you. Is it not so?"

The lad made no reply. But his silence was evidently the silence of assent. The stranger proceeded :—

"Think now, my young friend, what kind of a man does he propose to you to become? Such a one as himself, of course. Look at him, and think well whether you wish to be like him. You have heard him talk this evening, and probably at other times before this. You see that he already sneers at the holiest things on earth; scoffs at the purest affections of life; and betrays his familiarity with the foulest scenes under heaven. Poor sinner! My heart bleeds for him. So young! and yet such a profligate! Look on him, and consider well. If, while yet a boy, he has sunk so low, what will he be by-and-by?

"And *you*—should you conform to him now, in what condition would you find yourself a few years hence? Do you think you would be a man then?

"You have seen but little of the world yet, and much less of this New York world. But I have seen this thing carried out again and again. I have known more than I wish ever again to know, of lads who, in their haste to be men, sought to accomplish the end by the destruction of all the manliness which God has given us. I have had too many young friends who, like your companion, thought that the play houses, the billiard saloons, the gin shops, and viler haunts were the places for becoming men. I have seen them since; but they were not men. I have seen some of them among the wharf-loungers, and the bullies of the pit. I knew one—and he was a Pearl street clerk in his better days—to become a rag picker in the streets. I have known others who were pulled from the gutter into which they had been kicked from some low grog-shop. They were not men then: they were not near the glorious manhood which God bestows upon his creatures. I have known still others——*There! do you see that?*"

The speaker pointed to the figure of a female over the railing, bare-headed and bundled in rags, reeling along the Chambers street side-walk, asking the passers by for a sixpence, swearing horribly if it was refused, and then singing snatches of vile songs in shrill tones which sounded more fiendish than earthly.

The three stood a moment, silent gazers on the unsightly spectacle. Then Harfrant, attempting a coarse malicious raillery, inquired of the stranger if that also was one of his early friends. Unruffled by the sneer, the latter still addressed himself to Will.

"I am not aware," said he, "that I ever saw that poor creature before. For the honor of the sex, I can say farther, that I do not know that any female acquaintance of my own ever descended to a life of degradation. But when she passed, I was reminded of a woman whom I saw a few months ago, in a condition

just as revolting as hers, and concerning
whose history I was informed by a person
who knew it. She came from the theatre—
not from the parquet, family circle, or gal-
leries ; but from behind the scenes. What
iniquities would stand revealed, if we knew
all that is implied in that sentence—"behind
the scenes !" What a moral stench would
arise, if the cover were lifted from that steam-
ing caldron !

"Well," he added, "she was once an actress.
She was one of the divinities who were to lift
boys up into men ! She was the sorceress
who, with the aid of gin shops and billiard
saloons, could transform raw country lads into
accomplished New York gentlemen !

" Do not understand me," he added, " as
saying that every actress becomes low in the
common estimation of the world. Some of
them, they tell us, move in respectable society
to the last. Some have abandoned their
calling while young, and have secured esteem
for their domestic and social virtues.

" Still," he continued, ' it is a striking fact,
that, in numerous cases, we hear of them for
a few months or years, as stars in the theat-
rical firmament, and then they disappear.

3 *

What has become of them ?   The question is
asked, but nobody answers it.   Now if you
were to go with this young sinner, to the
National, you would see actresses there.   But
if you are wise, you will imagine that you
saw an actress just now, and you will say to
yourself, 'That will do!'"

He went on to say : " I was telling you of
early friends of my own, who thought that
the places of public dissipation would make
men of them.   Some of them are now in the
alms-houses and penitentiaries.   Last year I
went to the Tombs to see one of them.   He was
a condemned culprit.   As I left his cell, a
pale weeping woman, with a child on her arm,
entered.   It was his wife and son.   She had
come for their parting interview.   As the
fruit of his crime, she was now to become a
widow without a home, and that babe was to
grow up an orphan who could never think
without shame that he ever had a father.   The
next day he was executed, and his body was
tumbled into a felon's grave.

" Now," he continued, " think, on the one
hand, of those whom you have been accustomed to honor and revere.   Then think, on
the other hand, of those poor creatures, and

judge for yourself who are *the men.* Were
there not among the acquaintances of your
country home, virtuous and respected men,
who were trained to manhood without the aid
of cigars, rum, cards, or theatres? Perhaps
your own father was never at the theatre. Is
he not for you as noble a pattern of manhood,
as the blubbering vagabond in the station
house, whom the watch fished up from the
sewer? You have noticed the hale and happy-
looking old gentleman, who sits across the
aisle from you in church. New York has few
citizens who are held in higher esteem, or
who have been entrusted with more honors.
I have heard him say that, while all his days
have been spent in the city, he has never
crossed the threshold of a billiard saloon or
theatre. Which best meets your views of
what makes a man—this gentleman worship-
ping in the house of God, or the rag picker
with his hook, wading along the gutters?"

The speaker, pursuing his entreaty, became more and more compassionately earnest.

"My young friend," he said, "you must
not forget that you have an immortal soul. I
suppose, from what I heard said to you, that
there were religious influences in your home.

Is it manly to fling away those sacred influences? Is it manly to learn to sneer at the good, and to blaspheme the name of your Maker? Is it manly to glory in sins, over which the Redeemer of men wept, and to save men from which, he died? You may shudder now at the thought of such atrocity, but you will come to it if you begin. Your companion has done it all here to-night.

"God, in his word, has told you of the character and end of the way which you are urged to enter. He has told you that the dead are in such places; that they are the way to hell, going down to the chambers of death. He has told you that, if you perish in this way, you will 'mourn at the last, when your flesh and your body are consumed, and say, How have I hated instruction, and my heart despised reproof!' People here, as well as in the country, possess undying souls. Here, as well as there, those who die in Christ, die only to soar to the life and love of heaven. Here also the sinner who wears out a short life in sin, must pass to the realm of remorse and despair. What a fearful hour for the soul departing for that world! What a

sight of anguish for those who survive!
Before you decide to plunge into the torrent,
think once more of those you have loved—
those who love you all the more for every
long week of absence. Think that you see
them standing over your own shrouded
corpse, and mourning without consolation,
because there was no hope in your death."

* * * * * *

Long before the close of this appeal, Harfrant had left the scene. Will had remained
—whether willingly or reluctantly, it was
not then easy to determine. The fountain
of emotion was stirred: so much was evident.
Harfrant was probably lurking in the shade,
waiting to renew the attack as soon as the
track should again become clear.

The gentleman, on parting with him for the
evening, felt painfully apprehensive that the
strength of the conflict was not past. Often
on his homeward way, with alternating hope
and fear he asked of himself the question
which we have before asked,

"Will he be saved?"

PART II.

TWO ENTRIES IN MR. EMBREE'S DIARY.

September 30.—NIGHT is wearing away, but I write because my heart is too full for sleep. What more can be done for young men and boys from the country, thronging our city? They are sure to be surrounded by the vilest agents of perdition; but far enough from sure that even one kind and Christian arm will be extended to save them. Their peril is of late becoming the habitual anxiety of my soul. I think this is from God. I can *feel*, and I can *pray*. But the little I can *do*—Oh! it takes but a drop from this great New York ocean of need. We must have more effort, extensive, well organised, and all alive with the spirit of Jesus. At best there is only here and there a case which any one man, working all alone, can reach.

This evening I made a direct effort to pluck

one brand from the burning. For me it was a bolder move than usual. I was obliged to confront vice and hell in the very act of taking a fresh victim in their grasp. But the occasion was so providential, and the appeal to my Christian humanity was so mournfully strong, that I could not forbear. I believe, nay I am sure that I was called of God to it. *" Save with fear, pulling them out of the fire!"* It was God's message to me. No time was to be lost. Had I faltered, the blood of a lost soul might have been upon my conscience.

The issue is known only to God. But whatever that issue may be, I can now think of it without remorse. But I am anxious, painfully anxious still. The Providence which threw me into the way at the exact time, and the Spirit which first called me to the conflict, and then sustained me in it—can I accept these as a pledge that God means to use my labor of this night, as the poor instrumentality for saving a fair young character from the leprosy of our city corruptions, and an immortal soul from death?

This is the tone of my hope now, but I am oppressed still. The time for anxious effort and prayer is far enough from being over. I have hope that the immediate purpose of the tempter is baffled ; that the poor lad for whose rescue I made this abrupt interference, did not go into the theatre to-night. But what for the time to come? O God, provide! And if I have yet more to do in his behalf, teach me, and strengthen me!

This notion that virtue is childish and *green*, and that sin is the road to manliness—I believe that I have seen it work more ruin to young men than all other forms of temptation united. They are persuaded to swear and drink, to frequent the play houses and the resorts of dissipation, by being told that tenderness of conscience against these vices is puerile. There was not one original suggestion in all the seductive discourse which I heard this evening—nothing but what is heard over and over again in this city, and I suppose wherever else sin reigns—nothing but what is heard by almost every young man who lives in this world of wickedness.

It has been proved false in every way in which it is possible for falsehood to be brought to shame. The highways, the asylums for people whose career of vice is running its last dregs, the alms-houses, the prisons, the

grave, and the black realm beyond, are full
of examples that sin and manliness have no
partnership. The world knows it. Even the
victims of false shame know, while they seem
to be deceived, that they are sacrificing all
the sweetness of life here, and all their immortal hopes, to a shameful delusion. And
yet on and on they go.

What *does* it mean?

Alas! back of all these temptations from
without, lies their powerful auxiliary within
—the inborn corrupt nature which, until it
has been transformed by grace, is sure to
plead for sin, because it is on the side of sin.
There lies the secret of all this peril. There
the problem,———

"I know the right and yet the wrong pursue,"

———is solved.

There lies the peril of my new-found friend,
Will. His is a kind that goes not out except
by prayer and fasting. Something within
me bids me hold on to that lad—tells me,
"Thy life for his life, if thou let him go!" I
must fast and pray. While I write, he may
be in calm slumber, dreaming of his Fairstream home, forgetful of the events of the

4

evening; but all this unconsciousness makes his peril of body and soul none the less. I cannot sleep: my heart is full. I can only pray.

October 1.—Wonderfully in keeping with the events and reflections of the last evening, is a note which was sent in this morning. It invites me to attend a lecture on the quality of true manliness, gotten up for the special benefit of those just stepping into young manhood. It is to come from a speaker who takes his view from the stand-point of more than half a century of life, and who may therefore be supposed to know whereof he speaks. It will be delivered in the University chapel, next Sabbath evening.

I am requested to invite the attendance of any young friends, in whom I may feel a special interest. There are enough such. Will is certainly one of them. I must get into farther communication with him, and I must do it soon. Is not this a providential way of access?

Shall I also extend the invitation to the young scoffer, his early acquaintance? I may be told that it is casting pearls before swine : still it may place my own conscience more at ease.

But why is my soul so empty of hope when I think of him ? Older and viler sinners have been brought to the Saviour's feet. I call this to mind, and yet why is it that the heavens seem like brass, and faith is so shut up as by an invisible prohibition, when I attempt to pray for him ?

* * * * * * *

"A Lecture addressed to young men !" Well I am far enough from being one of those. But I am thankful that here in the autumn of life, there still remains in my heart enough of the glow of its glorious spring, always to inspire my interest in such a theme. I would not forget those days, for I expect by-and-by to renew my youth as the eagles. I expect all the sweet substantials of the May of life over again, in the world,

"Where everlasting spring abides,
And never withering flowers."

Jacob Embree has gray hairs, more than "here and there" upon him. But notwithstanding all that, he is booked for the lecture.

PART III.

THE LECTURE.

THE suggestions which I am now to prepare are offered especially to those who have just entered, or are just about entering the period of manhood. They are prompted by the reflection that, during those years of life, the aspiration for manliness of character is one of the highest elements of dread, or of hope. No tongue can speak the amount, either of good or wickedness, to which a youth of generous impulses may be incited, by the appeal, "Come, be a man!" or by the scornful taunt which denies his manhood, and tells him that he is out too soon from the nursery.

This strife for manliness is a great contest for a splendid prize. With correct views of the quality of that prize, it becomes one of the noblest of human ambitions. Those of us who have lived through more of life, and, from our longer experiences, better learned what it is really worth, often turn an earnest and fond look toward the generation behind us. It imparts a fresh glow to our own memories of young days, and secures the warm sympathy of our hearts, to see our youth girding themselves for a career which shall leave its mark on the chronicles of time. It is good to see humanity well aroused from that brutish contentment which has no aspirations for the present, and seeks for nothing to come. Human virtue finds one of its strongest earthly safeguards in the manly ambition, well understood and properly pursued. Thus understood and pursued, it is the path to such exaltation as honors him who treads it, and fulfils the hopes of those who watch, in trembling hope, for his future.

Young friends, I come to you now to cheer you forward in the race for this prize. Throngs of panting contestants are on the track, but there is still room for all. Run, for it is a glorious race!

But be sure that you run well. False goals and counterfeit prizes line the whole course, and all around them lie many high expectations of honor which have turned

4*

into shame; many lofty aspirations which have bitten the dust. Crowds of aspirants, who mistook the character of manliness, and adopted wicked means of reaching it, have found their aspiration to become the instrument of deep woe and disgrace in the present world, and eternal shame in the world to come. It is fearful to contemplate the immense power which the manly ambition is sure to wield over your coming character and destinies—power for good or evil; for the honors of earth and heaven, or for shame and everlasting contempt. It leads one along the path of serene virtue, and another through the slimy walks of sin, in pursuit of the prize. One is helped upward toward heaven, and another is driven down to perdition, under the all-thrilling appeal, " Be a man !"

The tempter, spreading his snare around the young, knows only too well the power of this high ambition, and its easy susceptibility of perversion. Sons of Belial ask you to go astray. They strive to make you think it noble to sin, and unmanly to obey God. They press you with sudden temptations, and allow you no time to think. They press you into public midnight carousals, or they invite you tɔ stealthy visits to the haunts of sin. They ask you to sit down at the gaming table where the atmosphere reeks with the fumes of cigars and brandy. No form of temptation which has corrupting power, is passed over. Your soul is the prize sought, and the ruin of this soul is the tempter's victory.

Your reluctance to yield may be strong. You may earnestly wish yourselves a thousand miles away from the peril. But the terrible appeal—"Will you be a puling babe, or a man?" falls like the bolt from a black cloud, upon your better feelings. God save you in that hour! for then is the time when many a young dupe of Satan is led "as a fool to the correction of the stocks, till a dart strike through his liver, as a bird hasteth to the snare, and knoweth not that it is for his life."

In a southwestern state, two men met to settle a hateful quarrel with weapons of death —in other words, to fight a duel. At the first fire, one fell into the arms of his second, strangely called his friend. He was mortally wounded, and well knowing it was so, he summoned the last strength of life to inquire— "Did I behave like a man?" "Yes," said his

second, "you behaved like a man." "Then,"
said he, "I die satisfied;" and thus, from the
field of suicide and murder, his soul went to
stand before its Maker.

Thus incitements as opposite and irrecon-
cilable as heaven and hell, approach the same
sublime quality in your nature—the one to
employ it for your glorious exaltation; the
other, for debasement and ruin. This lends
unspeakable interest to the questions, What is
true manliness? and, How shall it be reached?
You have seen enough of both the beginning
and ending of these things to admonish you
to beware how you yield any response to an
appeal to your manly ambition, until you have
well settled the great question, WHAT MAKES
THE MAN?

This inquiry faithfully pursued—especially
pursued in the light of the holy revelation
from heaven—will show to what earnest and
sanctified strifes in the race of ambition, the
consciousness of your immortal nature ought
to lead you. For you there read that such
of the traits of the manhood of our race as
make us men, in distinction from the brutes,
are no less than a gleam of Divinity within
us—a participation in the very nature of God.

One thought of this glorious heritage of your natures will settle the point, that the path to true manliness is a Godward path. It will stigmatize every ambition or act which loosens you from God, as a brutish assimilation, disrobing you of glorious manliness.

Though I have announced this conclusion in advance of all discussion, I shall not ask you to jump to it. In fact it will be the main purpose of my present effort, to inquire whether these things are so.

You nowhere read that God, in creating the lower orders of animals, such as the beasts and birds, gave to their inner natures anything that was Godlike. It is true those natures sometimes exhibit interesting traits, but they reveal no capacity for communion with the Divine nature. The brutes, in their best estate, are but brutes, and there is no hope of elevating their intellect to a point which contains one thought of God. So all voluntary forgetfulness of God, is an approximation to that nature.

When God took in hand a loftier achievement in the work of creation, he said, " Let us make *man* in *our image,* after *our likeness.*" It was not enough that he should be moulded in the nature of an angel, or made as the seraphs which glow in the brightness of the throne of heaven. Such a glory might seem illustrious enough for our conception, but it is a glory which pales before the sublimer dignity spoken in the history—" In the image of God created he him." It is again said, " God breathed into his nostrils the breath of life, and man became a living soul."

Thus humanity received its vitalizing element. So man stands related to the Highest Life in heaven. I have now no particular exposition to make of these remarkable accounts of the Divine origin of man. It is enough to say that you can give them no meaning but what should enkindle your self-respect, remind you that your nature is born of God's own, and show you that every removal from God is a descent into meanness.

Even heathen writers have caught up the theme of man as the child of Divinity; and it has furnished the matter for some of the grandest conceptions in their literature. Allow me, for example one quotation. It is from the Greek poet, Aratus. I venture the attempt of a metrical translation.

" Our living sense, our breath, our being, came
    From THE DIVINE, whom mortals ne'er may name.
    His unseen presence fills the silent lea ;
    The crowded haunts of men, the lakes, the sea,
    Are full of him.   And from his watchful care,
    Comes all our good, for we his offspring are."

I have repeated this, chiefly in view of the probable fact that it is the passage which the Apostle Paul had in mind, when he said to the Athenians, " Certain also of your own poets have said, ' For we are also his (God's) offspring.' "   It is but one out of a legion of accessible examples, in which the revelations of nature have united with those of the inspired Word, both together furnishing the largest induction for this great thought—a thought which should discipline the mind itself into greatness:—It is the Godlike in *man, that makes him a man.*

If our inquiry were to end here, the character of some attempts at manliness which are only too popular among certain classes of our youth, might be regarded as settled. In the streets of the city, or in places of public resort in the country, you see the young aspirant for these honors. He may be twenty-one, or he may be only fifteen years of age. He is tired of tutors and governors, and he feels it time to make a sensation on his own account. In his language, he affects an intimacy with the resorts of dissipation, and flings about the slang of sin. He glories to have it seen that he can walk unabashed and hardened to the fountain of drunkenness, and call for the cup with a speech and air which sneers at the sorrows of those who mourn for departing manhood and ruined souls.

Skill in profanity is another of his proud accomplishments. Since profanity is virtually a contempt of God publicly expressed, and since he regards the farthest remove from the restraints of religion as the highest sign of manhood, he has learned the familiar use of the most impious appeals to God, and the most awful imprecations of Jehovah's wrath. He would pity the lad whom he should hear conversing ten minutes, without some vile speech. He would set him down as one who had never seen the world outside of a praying home or a Sabbath-school, and who had all his manliness yet to gain.

You know the great extent to which, in this line of description, I might add point to point. I might speak of the loathsome and obscene tongue which utters fleshliness, sen-

suality, and devilishness.* I might especially
dwell upon that most hardened atrocity where
the sinner speaks contemptuously of the com-
passion with which the good follow him; in
some cases even deriding the sorrows of his
father and mother, whose best hopes he is
thus coolly trampling in the dust. And I
could make the description much more vivid,
by repeating some of the profane phrases
through which this loathsomeness of heart is
expressed. But God forbid that I should
ever spice a public address with language
which befits only a lower world than this!

If this be *manliness*, God give us brutishness
in its stead! For however low the brute may
be, he is always faithful to the scale in being
which he occupies. He is never unfaithfu
to his nature, while those of whom I have
spoken degrade our born humanity to sottish
ness. The brute will never mourn at the last

---

* A British naval Captain once ordered a midshipman on
deck, there in presence of the officers to have his mouth
cleansed with swab and brush. The operation of alternately
swabbing and rinsing was protracted until the poor fellow
roared for mercy. The Captain had overheard him using
language which violated decency, and he said that such a
mouth must be well cleansed before he could allow it to be
used in His Majesty's service, or in eating His Majesty's
rations.

5

when flesh and body are consumed, over in-
structions despised, and a soul lost. The
man who has voluntarily and persistently un-
manned himself, must do it.

Alas for hapless young adventurers on the
voyage for manhood, when they find themselves in a piratical ship where manliness was
only a false flag, soon to be lowered for the
running up of the black emblem which speaks
the real character of the cruise and the awful
work in hand !

But the question returns—What is true
manliness ?   A few moments back I gave you
the answer, but only in outline. This will
not meet your expectations, and I cheerfully
proceed to a more elaborate examination.

Then, young candidate for manhood, let me
refer you to some points in which you are un-
like and superior to the brute beneath you,
and in which you find your resemblance to
the God above you.

In bringing the subject into this light,
strange as you may think me, I would not
have you make too quick account of the
natural qualities of *reason* and *understanding*
—mere intellect ; or even of the heart's affections as they bear upon earthly beings around

you. There is a certain sense—a low sense it is true, but still a degree, in which these traits are possessed by the lower orders of animals. People who deny this, appear to me to walk blindly among the brutes; they make no accurate observation of their conduct.

The brute often chooses when some alternative is before him. He makes his choice in view of motives, and he makes it wisely also. He sometimes lays his plans with deliberation, and changes them as circumstances change. You see this in his management for taking his prey, or defending himself from his enemies. You see also that he remembers the relations of events, and when the occasion requires, he uses the remembrance with judgment. It is idle to ascribe all this to mere animal instinct. A mental process is going on, and in that process a kind of reason and judgment are employed.*

* I had the following incident from the lips of an old gentleman, whose character was such as to forbid my doubting his word. The smith, while shoeing his horse, drove a nail into what is called the quick of the foot. It was not immediately discovered, but it was not long before the animal became lame, and betrayed great suffering. He returned with him to the shoer, and had the badly driven nail drawn,

The brute has also what we call a heart—affections which are quick and ardent. Conjugal, parental and social attachments sometimes wonderfully strong dwell in that heart, prompting the most energetic actions which he ever performs. The mourning of Orpheus for Eurydice was not more plaintive than that of the turtle dove for his slaughtered mate. The bear bereaved of her whelps is a Scriptural emblem of the wrath of the Great Almighty himself. The lion defending his household makes the earth tremble under his roar; while, in that same lair, the maternal paw stirs the whelps with all the gentleness with which a human babe is laid on its pillow. The wolf-mother makes her most daring excursions when the wants of her young force

---

when the foot was relieved of pain. Some months afterward, at the same place, a like blunder was made in shoeing him. He was taken home and turned into the pasture. He soon began to suffer, and remembering how he was formerly relieved, he leaped the fence, returned alone to the smithy, walked to the shoeing stand, and raised his foot. He was understood and relieved.

I have myself seen a company of enraged swallows in the act of walling up a martin in the nest of which she had rifled one of their number. thus dooming her to perish in a living grave. It may have been barbarous, but it was certainly thoughtful.

her to the hunt. Instances are numerous in which brutes have died in defence of their offspring; and there are really affecting records of cases in which, under the agonies of death, they have bestowed their last strength in fond caresses of them. Here then are homes, and conjugal and parental loves; and yet it must be remembered that there is not a spark of the manly nature in it all.

Still, I would not have you make more of these phenomena than they really contain. Bringing first the intellect into the comparison, you find in the mind of man alone a certain something of the likeness and image of God, in which he was created—attainments which distinguish him, not merely in degree, but *radically*, from the brute. The understanding of a mere animal extends only to the small circle of subjects which relate to his animal wants. Sensuality bounds all his researches and attainments. You look to him in vain for any shrewdness, skill, or mental operation of any kind, beyond what is excited for the defence, sustenance, or pleasure of the purely sensual nature. In all the brute kingdom, there is not the first ray of an aspiring intellect. Not one of that race has ever betrayed a desire for knowledge for its own sake, or a longing for any higher art than what promotes sensual gratification.

But you have a mind which, if you do not yourself sensualize it, is ever soaring above this fleshly range of thought. This experience forms one of the signatures of your superior nature. When you summon all your mental energies to think great thoughts, to plan for noble achievements, and to sustain persevering efforts for their attainment, then you reveal the Godlike in yourself. True, it is a much lower revelation of the celestial nature than others which I shall hereafter notice: still it is a real and exalted manifestation of it.

There is much which I would say, just here in the way of suggestions for your ambition and conduct, were it not that time presses, and other points of yet higher moment lie before me. In this connection, I can only warn my young friends who are ambitious to become men, that they must learn to think as true men think. In intellect as well as in outward habits, they must cast off both foppishness and sensuality. They must find some richer themes for conversation than neck ties,

waltzes, cigars, prima-donnas, and pretty faces. I have said that the intellect of the
brute is void of the quality of aspiration.
But before the immortal mind, God has in-
scribed, in blazonry of fire, the watchword,
"EXCELSIOR!" The life of the soul is a real
and earnest life. Its intellectual ambition
should be for growth upward, even to celestial vigor. It is an ambition from which race,
profession, or social position, excludes no human being. The strife is open to all, and the
rivalry for the highest award, is one in which,
as said by the old Grecian bard, "there is
glory to the victor, and no dishonor to the
vanquished."

Next making *the heart's affections* the
point of comparison, let me caution you that,
for the present, I speak of them simply as
natural traits, without reference to their holiness or unholiness. This clear and funda-
mental distinction lies between the merely
animal and the manly nature:—The brute
has manifestly no constitutional powers for
love beyond a contracted sphere. The circle
of his attachments is limited, and toward all
beyond it, he is either indifferent, or fero-
ciously hostile.

But you have a nature large enough to love a whole world of the creatures of God, and to find neighbors and brethren, bone of your bone and flesh of your flesh, in every clime under heaven. You can look upon all the sorrows of the world, and welcome to your heart a living sympathy with every sufferer. You can lift up your voice, and employ every practical appliance which you possess, against all the wrongs which load our world with misery. You can go, a messenger of love to the hovels of poverty and beds of sickness. In short, wherever your self-denying charities can give joy in the place of sorrow, there you can illustrate the superior character of the human affections. Let it be yours to show that they are not circumscribed by family affinities, or race, but that, like God's own, they have the wide earth for their sphere, and all who live on the earth for their objects!

Young friends, I shall now ask you to step upward with me into the higher regions of this discussion. Approaching the more solemn traits of manliness, I point you, for one of them, to *the conscience within you.*

In the breast of the brute, there is no moral sense—no felt right and wrong. He shuns nothing simply because it is sinful; he does nothing because it is right.

But in your bosom, God has planted conscience as an eternal principle, never, *never* to be extinguished. It is true it may be almost stifled by a life of sin, and the sinner may harden himself to the point where he does not exhibit one sign of remorse. But this is only the slumber, and not the death of conscience. The time for the awakening comes, and then this Divine witness becomes an aroused scorpion for the guilty soul.

Oh, that each of my youthful friends knew the eternal value of his conscience! Cherish it, remembering that just in proportion as its influence is neutralized, you lose a powerful security against the deepest abandonment. Nourish your conscience as the mother nourishes her child. It was born within you of heaven—given from God to become your celestial guardian through a life of exposure to temptation. There can be no deeper degradation of your manhood than the attempt to sear, as with a hot iron, this Divine mark written on your nature—to wipe out this everlasting memorial of the heavenly nobility of your birth.

Another of the Divine signatures of your manly being, consists in this :—It is an existence which, like that of God *can never be extinguished.*

In what we call the mind of the brute, you look in vain for a single sign of immortality. Living only for the animal nature, he needs little observation, and still less study. And so all that he has to learn is soon learned ; and it is then evident that no addition to his term of life, not even an eternity of existence, would give any material increase to the measure of his attainment.

But those who observe the working of the human intellect, from infancy to old age, cannot fail to notice how little instinct does for it, and how slowly knowledge comes in through observation, experience, and reflection. And yet, with all the mind's slowness of attainment, there is no limit to its aspirations for knowledge and its capacity for acquisition. Through the longest life on earth, there are always investigations to be pursued, and points to be settled. In the common arts of life ; in what concerns every business and every profession ; in practical inventions ; in philosophy ; in moral science ; in theology—

in none of these things, nor, in short, on any
subject belonging either to earth or heaven,
can we instruct any man to his perfect satisfaction. You can name no science which is
not loaded with text books from the hands of
the best masters, and yet every teacher feels
his need of something better. There is
always some error to be corrected, some new
question to be asked, or some unfinished idea
to be carried out.

On all these facts concerning our race,
the great truth is emblazoned that the
human mind never reaches maturity. Its
work is never ended. The universe has
myriads of wonders which we have never
seen, yet long to explore. It contains deep,
fearful and eternal truths which we tremble,
yet pant to approach. This tendency of the
mind toward unlimited enlargement of both
capacity and knowledge, shows it forth as
the possessor of the dread, yet glorious attri-
bute of *immortality*.

Yes, young aspirants for manliness, immortality is the crowning gift of your manly
being! When God breathed into you the
breath of life, you became each a *living* soul,
not in the sense in which the brute lives for

a day or more, but in the more wondrous and
Diviner sense in which your Creator himself
lives—living a life incapable of extinction.
When therefore, after contemplating those
noble mental and moral faculties which have
been mentioned as interwoven in the struc-
ture of your being, you finish the view with
this highest one of eternal duration, then you
read the sublime truth, written on your im-
perishable nature as with God's hand-writing
of fire, that

THE SOUL MAKES THE MAN.

In the light of this truth, you have before
you the whole lesson in the study of manliness.   It is very simple, but how solemn!——
*In your reflections and your whole manner of
life, treat yourself as the possessor of an immortal soul.*

This lesson in manliness is more serious
because it is to be learned by those who have
lost the noblest part of inheritance in the
Godlike nature, through the fall of our whole
race from original holiness, and the conse-
quent propensity to sink the man into the
brute.   There can be no doubt that the highest part of the image of God, in which man

first came from the hand of his Maker, con-
sisted in full participation in the holiness
which reigns in heaven—in those perfectly
sinless affections which live warm in every celestial bosom. And the everywhere known
facts respecting human nature and conduct
are so entirely consonant with the testimony
of Holy Scripture, that the truth is just as
unquestionable, that, through the apostacy
of our race, every spark of this highest hea-
venliness was lost from the human breast. In
Eden, before the fall, there dwelt a *man*—one
who was every inch a man in the image of
God. Since the awful rebellion of the race,
the world has witnessed in sinful man no proper illustration of the true manliness, except
from the re-creating power of the atonement
through which "the second Adam restores the
ruin of the first."

Thus this great subject of manliness, by
its own inevitable tendings, works itself into
the shape of an earnest Christian counsel. It
bids you approach the throne of heaven in
true sorrow for sin, in the trusting faith which
gives the whole soul to Jesus Christ for mercy,
and with a heart which consecrates all, yourself included, to God. It tells you of this

6

as the first effectual step toward the Godlike
in humanity which formed the first glory of
manhood, which was again illustrated in the
human life of our Divine Redeemer, and without which our race can never become more
than the wrecks of men.

One feature out of the many which consti-
tute the superior grade of such manliness is
this:—Led by the inwrought work of the
Spirit of God, opening new views of the great
end of living, and new thoughts of the vile-
ness of sin and the beauty of holiness; im-
parting also new affections toward God and
all his creatures, and in short leading you
forth into a new life, you become self-conse-
crated to the noblest enterprises which ever
command human energies. You then say to
yourself:—"Did Christ indeed spend the life
which he lived in the flesh, to exalt such a
soul as mine into life and fellowship with
God? Did he turn coldly away from all in-
ferior ambitions, and devote the youth and
whole life of his incarnate existence to this
mission of love? Then let me share the
same spirit; let me aspire to this heavenly
example. Let it become the glory of my
emulation, and the business of my life, to

bless the world which sin has cursed, and to seek and save the lost. I cannot begin this work too early: I cannot follow it with an overwrought tenderness or faithfulness.

In this state of feeling, Divine love becomes the grace which prompts every labor, and sustains you under every self-denial. It is breathed from your heart; it dwells on your lips, and it glows from your life. Living the life of Jesus, in comforting the disconsolate, helping the poor, bearing with the wicked, praying for men, and doing your utmost to lead the world to heaven, you are all the while tracing views of human greatness upon the records of your generation, which will point out to survivors the path to the most illustrious manliness, when you are in your graves. The teaching of your example, and the influence of your lives, will become a fresh revelation of the truth that the true man is the man of God; or, as it has been elsewhere said,

" The Christian is the highest style of man."

My young auditors must allow me, in closing this theme, to assume an earnest tone. I think of the most solemn part of your existence as yet lying before you. This is true whether you die young or old. The most happy or miserable events of your being await your future experience, and the price of all is now in your hand.

We have seen the disgraceful issues of mistaken and corrupt ambition. We have seen that the courses to which sin invites you, when it affects to rouse your manliness, are such as spur only the sensual nature into action. Just in proportion as this preponderates, the soul is degraded. As the brute rises within you, the man sinks. Then seeking for yourself the manliness which is such in the fair estimation of all worlds, look to your undying soul, and secure for that the inheritance of glory, and the eternal life of God. Sinful human nature can find no attitude so dignified as when the penitent lays himself before the cross, and there raises his cry for mercy and cleansing. For only there he becomes clothed in the moral likeness of which sin despoiled us, and which was our constituent participation in the heavenly nature. Poor humanity never rose more surely from its ruin, than when the sorrowing sinner washed her Saviour's feet with her tears, and wiped them with the hair of her head. For then the soul began to shine in the restored glory of heaven. Those tears were the sparklings of a nature which had plumed itself for the everlasting ascent. In contrast, the splendors which surrounded the feast of the scorning Pharisee were the circumstances of a day: to-morrow the pang which they were sure to leave behind would be almost their only memorial.

Young candidate for manhood, you scorn the thought of passing a driveller through the world, unfelt while you live, and missed by none when you are gone. This is right. Who could wish his track through life to be only that of the ship on the ocean, where the waters close in upon its wake, smoothing over all trace of its passage the instant that passage is made? You wish to become the author of noble achievements, and in dying, to bequeath to the world living memorials that you have been here among men. This again is right.

But could you even surpass all renown of human achievements: could you, in mere temporal creations, even match yourself with God and reach out your hand and garnish

6 *

these lower heavens with worlds of light, placing planetary systems in their fields, and sending comets along their mysterious paths in the regions of space, it would be as nothing to what you may now do to show the grandeur of those powers which crown our race with glory and honour. It is more ennobling to fold your soul in the robe of your Redeemer's righteousness. For the glory of those physical creations would only be temporal. Every sun and star would expire in the ruin of all things below heaven. But the greatness of the soul committed to Christ is the greatness of the Divine nature, coeval henceforth with the existence of God. Aspiring only to the renown of goodness, while the Christian is on his passage to the skies, there is growing up for him on earth a name which shall be like the cedar of Lebanon.

I have no words—language itself has no words to express the interest which belongs to such terms as *youth—early hopes—morning hours of life.* The mind which comprehends all that is here implied, reels under the weight of the thought.

Those of us who are older, often live in the memory of days like yours. In the vision of our past, there are sprightly forms, laughing faces, bounding aspirations, and hoping hearts.

But the groups, the songs, the friends, the lovers, and the ambitions of our young days —where are they now? Many a voice of merriment has ceased, and many a harp lies unstrung among the rubbish of a former generation.

Our experience is in the main to beome yours—the experience of the uncertainty of all youthful hopes from the world. Among your present society, disappointments and death will tame earthly ambitions, and the wild throbbings of worldly excitements will become still. Soon those who survive, and look about among the scenes of their youth, inquiring for the friends of early days, will find more monuments of the dead than forms of the living. Should it then be found that no higher record remains for the eye of the survivor than that of earthly achievement and human greatness, how short will be its passage to oblivion!

The memorials of a holy Christian consecration live on. This secures the everlasting remembrance promised to the just. Restored from the fallen image of the first man,

PART IV.

AT HOME.

TWELVE years have passed since the occurrence described in our opening pages. They are years in which, as in all the times of earth,

"Change and chance are busy ever."

The scene, as well as the years are changed. We have left the great Babel, New York, on the face of which both the best and the worst of earth is photographed; and we stand, with our portfolio, in one of the lusty young cities of the North-West.

We look in upon a family group in a pleasant home, which, within and around, bears the marks of thrift and refinement. The group itself consists of a young couple, with their infant child, and a gentleman whose snow white hair speaks the old man, but

PART IV.

AT HOME.

TWELVE years have passed since the occurrence described in our opening pages. They are years in which, as in all the times of earth,

"Change and chance are busy ever."

The scene, as well as the years are changed. We have left the great Babel, New York, on the face of which both the best and the worst of earth is photographed; and we stand, with our portfolio, in one of the lusty young cities of the North-West.

We look in upon a family group in a pleasant home, which, within and around, bears the marks of thrift and refinement. The group itself consists of a young couple, with their infant child, and a gentleman whose snow white hair speaks the old man, but

whose undimmed eye, together with the active
workings of his countenance, tell that his bow
abides in strength.   He is the father of the
lady.

It is a winter evening.   The old gentleman
is quietly looking over the paper which has
just come to hand.   His daughter, Mrs.
Woodfall, has her babe on her lap and some
light sewing in her hand.   Her husband has
just sat down, and is chirping a smile from
the little one.

"A feather in your cap, Will!"

The old gentleman raised the paper as he
spoke, thereby intimating that he had there
made the discovery.

Mr. Woodfall turned from his infant, and
looked inquiringly toward the speaker—as
much as to say, "A what?"

"A feather in your cap! I say," the other
repeated.   "Do you understand, my boy?"

The young man suggested that it was rather difficult to understand what he knew nothing about.   But the curiosity of his wife
was more thoroughly aroused.   She appealed
eagerly to her father for explanation.

"Oh I dare say *you* would like to know,"
he said.   "Catch a daughter of Eve quiet,

especially if anything is on foot for her husband."

This of course was tantalizing, though meant only to be sportively so. But there was that in her countenance at that moment, which swept his memory through the years gone to the evenings of his own young married life, when her mother sat by his side, and gave her whole soul's interest to any thing which might bring favor or happiness to him. Such recollections chastened his feelings while he proceeded to state the purport of his discovery. It was simply this, that in a communication to Congress, made by the Secretary of the Treasury, special notice had been taken of the official capacity and services of Mr. Woodfall.

The color mounted to the face of the latter, as he inquired with an earnestness which spoke emotion, " Is the document there?"

" There pa !" said Mrs. Woodfall, " you see there is a *son* of Eve who wants to know something."

" To be sure, Julia !" said her husband. " I should think no better of myself if I were too calm to feel excitement from commendation, especially if it comes from a quarter where it is honorable to be mentioned. You know the care and toil which I have bestowed on my trust. Self-approval has been my best reward, and I expect no better from man. But there is no human nature above feeling the desire for a recognition of faithful service on the part of those who have been served."

The old gentleman now remarked that the document referred to was not spread out in the paper before him—the Daily National Intelligencer—but there was an editorial notice of it. He then read the notice as follows :—

" A special communication from the Treasury Department, relating to the affairs of the Land Agencies, was yesterday morning sent in to both Houses of Congress. It contains statements in detail of the management of the business of the various offices, and affords a better view of the fitness of the respective incumbents than we generally obtain from such a paper.

" We are pleased to see that Mr. Woodfall, who is at the head of the——District, is singled out for special commendation. This is a distinction which that officer has fairly earned. True he has seen but two years of service, but they

have been years of no light accomplishments
His district is a very important one, and, pre-
vious to his assuming the charge of it, its revenues had fallen off, and its affairs gone into
almost inextricable confusion.   All this is
now changed.   Business talent put into
prompt and energetic execution, has done
what may always be expected of it.   Chaos
has been reduced to order, and the affairs of
the agency, revenues included, now give the
government the highest satisfaction.

"We are more pleased to record this, because it encourages the right kind of appoint-
ments to fiscal offices—that of men whose ta-
lents lie in that direction, in preference to
those who claim the places as the reward of
political services.   Mr. Woodfall was not an
applicant for the office.   He was brought to
the notice of the New York delegation in
congress as a young man who had received a
first class business training; who had proved
himself a skillful financier; who, for his years,
had exhibited unusual ripeness of judgment;
whose moral principle was strong, and whose
life was incorrupt.   As such they placed his
name before the President, at a time when
the condition of the office in question de-

manded a man of that stamp. It is true his want of experience did seem to render the appointment a little hazardous: but the maturity required was the maturity of judgment, rather than of years. In the former he has been tried, and not found wanting. The country has reaped the benefit of a selection made on such principles. Mr. Woodfall has secured the confidence of both the government and the people with whom he has had to deal. He deserves to rise, and we expect to see him rise. We have no doubt that higher trusts await him—that more important services for the country lie in his path."

Probably the reader has already recognized in Mr. Woodfall, the "Will" of that perilous scene of temptation in the rear of the City Hall, recorded in our first chapter. I may as well state here that, in the person of his venerable father-in-law, we are renewing our acquaintance with Mr. Embree, the stranger Christian friend who appeared so unexpectedly in that scene, striving to save the young man from a dangerous companion, and from his own false shame.

From what has just appeared, the result of that earnest effort of Christian love may easily be guessed. Will did not go to the theatre with his fellow boarder; neither did he accompany him to those other resorts of dissipation then named, along the same wide thoroughfare to hell. The door of "Barker's," which it appears he had twice entered, he never again darkened.

And yet, in spite of the taunts of his tempter, *he became a man.* While many whose standing and advantages at the first were equal to his own, lived only to loll about the drinking houses, or bet on the muscle of low prize fighters, he stepped into his place as the companion of the virtuous and honored of earth.

On the eventful evening first named, Mr. Embree, as already seen, had left him, painfully uncertain respecting the issue of the struggle. But he had fixed his eye upon him as one whose salvation was to become the burden of his own soul. He beheld him as a lamb out of the fold, and for himself there was henceforth to be no rest until that lamb should be folded, and thus secured from the howling wolves all around him. He im proved the earliest opportunity for fuller acquaintance with him, and then learned with

delight that his first opportune effort to ex-
tricate him from the toils of false shame had
not been in vain. The appeal of this unex-
pected friend, coming as an angel from
heaven might have come, to poor Will, in the
hour when he knew not what to do, turned
the scale for that one night of conflict; and the
decision of that night turned the whole course
of events with him for all the life to come.

Who can measure the amount of present
and eternal happiness which has grown out
of words fitly spoken—fitly in regard to time
as well as character? On the other hand,
what arithmetic is there to compute the
agonies which have been endured because no
hand was stretched out in the hour of extreme
peril? The young victim, left alone of man
in the hour of conflict with temptation, and
having never learned to look to Heaven for
help—what is he to do? Refuge fails him;
no man cares for his soul. Every friend of
goodness has daily opportunities for doing
for others substantially what Mr. Embree did
for Will. "Go thou and do likewise."

Soon after this commencement of their acquaintance, Mr. Embree had the satisfaction
of introducing his newly acquired young

friend to a Bible class; and before a year had expired, he went up with him to the Holy Supper of our Lord. He also took upon himself the charge of a class in a missionary Sunday-school under the superintendence of his faithful Christian friend, and became his earnest co-worker in the whole round of Christian service to which the life of this good man was so largely devoted. There are now many living monuments of this gentleman's successful interposition between tempted youth and their ruin; but he won no conquests of this kind from which he obtained greater satisfaction than he found in William Woodfall.

The daughter of Mr. Embree—a young lady in all respects worthy of the father—gradually became a partner in the intimacy which had sprung up between Will and her father. This after a few years, resulted in her accepting the relation to the young man, in which we now find her. When the latter received the appointment which required their removal to the West, it was agreed that her father should accompany them, and that they should permanently remain one family. He had buried his other children, and finally

7*

followed his wife to the grave. Julia alone
remained of his family, and it behooved him to
abide with her until death should separate
them.

The reading of the notice which the government had bestowed upon Mr. Woodfall,
naturally led to a conversation that carried
them over the ground which they had passed
in each other's company, and the steps by
which the young man had reached his present
position. A portion of this conversation will
be recorded as affording a little further illustration of the false and true paths to manliness. Mr. Woodfall had just referred to the
companion in whose company he was first
found by Mr. Embree.

"That poor lad," said Mrs. Woodfall,—
"what finally became of him? I have heard
you say that he turned out badly; but how?
Had he a mother?"—and there was a slight
convulsion in the arm which held her infant,
that drew it closer to her bosom while she
asked the question, "Had he a mother?
Had he a pious home in his young days?
Did he fall into open disgrace? Is he living
now?"

"Alas Julia!" said her husband, "it is

a sad story for a heart like yours.   You ask
questions fast, and they are all sore ones to
answer. There is little to be said of the
details of Harfrant Symmes' progress to ruin,
but what might be said of almost any one who
is in the same road.   The theatre and all those
leprous establishments which flourish in its
atmosphere, afford but little variety in the
history of their victims.   One clerk or ap-
prentice may be expelled from his situation
for dissolute habits; another may be detected
in some dishonest practice to obtain the
means of dissipation, and be quietly sent
home to his friends; another may become so
skillful at the gaming table that he voluntarily
leaves his place to adopt the life of a profes-
sional gambler; and still another may break
open his employer's desk, and abscond with the
contents.   He may be arrested and sent to
the state prison, or he may never be heard
of again.   There may be a few such things
in which one case differs from another, but
the general story is the same.   They all
travel one way; it is down, down, down; and
when the bottom is reached, then comes the
end."

"Yes," said Mr. Embree, with deep

solemnity in his tone—"Yes, their end! their end! 'Until I went into the sanctuary of God ; then understood I their end.'"

Woodfall resumed :—

"After Harfrant found his attempts to draw me into his own associations unsuccessful, I saw less of him. Indeed he abandoned me entirely as soon as he found me really interested in the subject of religion, and offering reasons from the Word of God why I could not follow him to his vicious resorts."

"Aye," said Mr. Embree, "You may be sure enough of that. The sinner could not stand long before the Bible. Meet Satan himself with it, and he will turn pale. I have known many boasting scorners in my day, who were proud to contend where the contest was one of wit against wit, and argument against argument; but I have seldom seen one who did not cower before a Bible. They fear the Bible in the pulpit; they fear it in the hands of the colporteur ; they fear it in the public school ; and they hate the Sabbath school because the Word of God is there made the text book for holy instruction. The bare sight of a Bible is sufficient to put an army of them to flight. And well they may be dis-

mayed when that is brought into the field!
When they stand up before human arguments,
they meet only men. But from the Bible
God speaks, and before the voice of his
Maker, the scoffing sinner is abashed."

Woodfall again took up his narration :—

" Harfrant's time of trial at length came.
His excesses laid him on a bed of sickness,
and his physician told him that he must die.
Then I saw him again, but may God spare
me from another sight like that! His face,
permanently crimsoned by his habitual stimu-
lants, now, under the raging fever, appeared
in my imagination like burning anthracite.
His look was haggard; his eye had a fright-
ful glare, and all his motions were convulsive.
His cries for the mercy of God ring in my
ear to this day. He plead for life; he promised amendment; he sent solemn warnings
to his companions in iniquity, and said that
if God would only spare his life this once, he
would walk in their ways no more.

" To the astonishment of all he lived, and
slowly recovered. As soon as he was able to
be moved, he was carried to the home of his
parents in the country, and he remained there
several months. During that time I had oc-

casional correspondence with him. His let-
ters were not all which I could have wished,
but he constantly affirmed that he was con-
tented and happy in his return to regular
habits, and felt more and more resolved to
pursue them through life. I also learned
with great pleasure, that his friends looked
upon him as a thoroughly reformed young
man."

"Did this reformation endure?" inquired
Mrs. Woodfall.

"Ask him," said her father, "whether the
young man afforded evidence that he had received the true grace of God into his soul.
That will tell the story. 'Can the Ethiopian
change his skin, or the leopard his spots?
then may ye also do good, that are accustomed
to do evil.'"

Woodfall continued:—

"Harfrant at length returned to the city,
but he had been there some weeks before I
heard of it. This of itself was a suspicious
circumstance. My heart sank within me
when I heard how long he had been in New
York without my knowledge. I knew that
some change for the worse had taken place;
else he would have hastened to me. I called

on him.   He treated me with outward civility;
but it was plain that my acquaintance had
once more ceased to be agreeable to him.

"From that time I seldom saw him, but I
heard more of him than I wished.   The evil
spirit had returned to him with seven other
spirits more wicked than himself, and again,
but with frightfully increased momentum,
his course was down, down, down.   He was
discharged from his employment, and opened
a low groggery on the wharf.   There, as
might be expected, he was surrounded by a
horde of blear-eyed associates, whose hands
he would have scorned to touch in his better
days.

"At this period," continued the speaker,
"my heart was moved to make one more effort to save him.   With much difficulty I once
got him where we were alone.   I cannot tell
you all that I said, but I am sure I poured
out the fullness of a heart that was troubled
for his soul.   I know that I endeavored to
carry his memory back to the better things
of early days.   I spoke to him of eternal
happiness and misery, and of Christ the Saviour, who was yet able to pull him out from
the mire of sin.   He heard for a while with

cool indifference, but when Christ was pressed
upon his attention, his eye looked angry, and
his language became profane."

"I can believe that only too easily," said
Mr. Embree. "I have generally found it one
of the marks of apostacy from Christian instruction, that the cross becomes the central
point for a black, implacable hate. That cross
has always been the chief target for the mis-
siles of infidelity. Denunciation, sophistry and
jest, are most thickly launched against God's
most loving dispensation to earth; and the
noblest gift of Heaven is held in the vilest
esteem. When I see men falling off from a
Christian education into unbelief, I am fright-
ened. I see what is before them. It will
not suffice their spiritual temper to despise
religion in general. They will single out
Christ for their darkest malignity, and treat
the best of the gospel with their most studied
scorn. Yes, my boy, I have no doubt he was
mad, when you spoke to him of Christ. It
was awful, but it is the way such things go."

Woodfall's narrative proceeded:—

"I reserved, for my last effort, a review
of the well-remembered hours of his sickness.
I reminded him of those fearful cries for

mercy, and those promises of amendment. I strove to set before him the tenderness of the influences of the Divine Spirit, and the hopeless doom of those from whom the Holy Ghost departs. Then his eye glared with rage, and with a maddened tongue he reviled and cursed those hours of the Spirit's striving. Then I left him, for how could I hope any longer?*

"The worst part of his history followed, but do not ask me to relate it. He had blasphemed the Holy Spirit, conscious of what he was doing, and of course you can learn nothing more that is fit to be known."

"Oh horrible! horrible!" groaned Mrs. Woodfall: "*had* he a mother?"

"Yes," said her husband, "he had a father, mother, and sisters."

"Did it not kill them?"

"I paid them a short visit," said Woodfall, "near the time of which I last spoke. There I learned that his mother had more fears about his return to New York, after his sickness, than his other friends had. They felt strong confidence that he would do well now, but her heart was heavy. The news of his late misconduct had reached them before my

* Matthew xii. 31, 32.

8

visit, and Mrs. Symmes was then sick, and
unable to leave her room. Her physician
was there, and when he left, I walked with
him to the gate, and asked him respecting the
prospect of her recovery. He shook his head.
I inquired respecting her disease. 'There is
nothing,' said he, 'which belongs to our science: if there were, I should know what to
do. But we have no prescriptions for a broken heart, and the woman will probably die.'
I ventured to suggest that God has medicines
for such cases, and that, under his healing
hand, her restoration was yet possible. 'Yes,'
said he, 'nothing is too hard for the Almighty; but, young man, do you not know
that God often employs *death* as the healer
of those who are too sorrowful to live?'

"I mused upon the thought while he rode
away, and somehow the conviction grew up
in my mind that Mrs. Symmes would die.
The grass has since grown over her grave.
I have read the lines traced by the hand of
love upon the head-stone of that grave, but
my mind was more upon a sentiment which
the chisel had failed to record, viz. that the
young man whose misconduct has broken the

heart of a parent, is, in the sight of God, a parricide."

There was a short pause in the conversation, and then Mrs. Woodfall inquired :—

"Did the parents of Harfrant Symmes do right in allowing him to be exposed so young to New York city temptations ?"

"I think not," said her husband.

"And I think not," said Mr. Embree. "At least, if I am correctly informed, no sufficient cause existed for so early an escape from the restraining influences of home."

Mrs. Woodfall again drew her infant closer to her bosom, and said in such language and tone as a mother uses with her babe— "The precious little darling ! The bad folks shall never take *him* away from his mother —shall they ?"

A tear rose to the eye of the father while he devoutly said, "I hope not."

"My children," said Mr. Embree, "God will indeed be good to you, if he so orders your circumstances that you can afford your child the necessary preparation for usefulness, and still keep him under your own eyes until the proper time for self-government arrives. In this country, it is a privilege which com-

paratively few families enjoy.   The mere act
of sending abroad a child of tender age cannot properly be condemned, until the circumstances of the case have been considered.
Some parents *must* allow their children to go
from home, or keep them in ignorance.
Others have no means at hand for preparing
them for the business of life.   However
much such examples as that of Harfrant may
excite their alarm, they are straitened to the
painful alternative between the present
security and the future good of the child.
The question which shall be chosen, is the
most trying one of their whole domestic experience.   With some melancholy exceptions,
home is the safest place for a child, and if
he leaves home, it should be because the
necessities of the case drive him forth. When
there is no greater reason for his going than
his manifest desire to be his own governor,
the point of duty is clear.   The reason which
prompts his wish to go, is of itself conclusive
proof that he is not fit to receive the trust of
self-control.

"And," continued the speaker, "even
where a strong necessity does require the
separation, no child should be sent abroad

without some security for his morals beyond himself. This should be one of the first considerations in the selection of the place where he is to dwell, and the family with whom he is to live. Some friend should be sought out to stand to him in the place of a father, and he should be brought under direct and earnest religious influences. Without some of these guarantees, especially the last, he should never be allowed to depart from his natural home. Cases where home influences are corrupt, and where the present and eternal welfare of a child demand his removal, are of course exceptions to what I have said. But in such cases, what can be done? Philanthropy may weep over the question, but can wisdom answer it?

"As a general rule," he went on to say, "the departure of a boy permanently from his home is a perilous movement. Even when justified by the necessities of the case, it is still perilous. But it becomes most fearful when it is not fairly necessary. If he has a good country home, it is especially desirable that he should be allowed to grow up under its influence. If his restiffness under the restraints of home, and his desire

8 *

to outstrip the regular march of nature towards manhood, urge him away, then still deeper danger attends his removal. If he is sent to the great city unguarded, and left to form his associations for himself, it is most fearful of all. I have been told that each of these things was true in the case of Harfrant Symmes, and therefore I concurred in your remark, Will, that his parents ought not to have allowed him to go. I may seem rigid in my views of these things, but let people see what I have seen, and they will be of my mind. Even now my brain sometimes reels, and I am almost wild with the recollection of the sin and misery which I have known to come upon unguarded youngsters, far from home, and farther from God."

A brief silence followed his remarks. While Mr. Embree had spoken, the head of Woodfall had become bowed. Strong emotions were awakened in his soul. He too had, in the same tender years, left a good country home. It was true that self-government was not exactly the thing to which he then aspired: still he was conscious that there had been quite ambition enough to get along fast. Without sufficient care for his good oversight, he had been allowed to take a step which was surrounded with hazards that his soul now shuddered to review. As a son he had no heart to raise the question whether his own parents had done right, but he knew that he was a brand plucked from the burning.

The silence was broken by his wife who had read his thoughts. Thinking of him, of herself, and of their infant, she said :—

"What a world of happiness awaited the decision of that night when your soul 'escaped as a bird out of the snare of the fowler!'"

"True, my dear Julia," he replied: "I have marked that as 'a night to be much observed unto the Lord.' I regard it as forming the apparent turning point in my history, and I never think of it without consciousness of a debt of gratitude to your father, which oppresses me with its weight."

"No my son, not a debt of gratitude to *me*," said Mr. Embree; and he solemnly raised his eyes upward while he spoke.

"I know," Woodfall replied—"I do not forget that. Still I feel that I owe to *you* also what language cannot express, and how can I help it?"

he plead with God for poor and unguarded
youth, for whom Satan and his agents are
watching. He invoked the blessing of the
Spirit of wisdom and success upon all those
Christian laborers who enter the highways
and by-ways of sin, to seek and save the
lost.

It was his good custom to close his supplications with the form of prayer taught by
our Lord. In doing so at this time, he repeated a second time, with slow and solemn
emphasis, the petition:—

"LEAD US NOT INTO TEMPTATION, BUT DE-
LIVER US FROM EVIL."

THE END.

WS - #0060 - 130423 - C0 - 229/152/5 - PB - 9780243953035 - Gloss Lamination